PEANUTS.
TREASURY

Books by Charles M. Schulz

Peanuts
More Peanuts
Good Grief, More Peanuts!
Good Ol' Charlie Brown
Snoopy
You're Out of Your Mind, Charlie Brown!
But We Love You, Charlie Brown
Peanuts Revisited
Go Fly a Kite, Charlie Brown
Peanuts Every Sunday
It's a Dog's Life, Charlie Brown
You Can't Win, Charlie Brown
Snoopy, Come Home
You Can Do It, Charlie Brown
We're Right Behind You, Charlie Brown
As You Like It, Charlie Brown
Sunday's Fun Day, Charlie Brown
You Need Help, Charlie Brown
Snoopy and the Red Baron
The Unsinkable Charlie Brown
You'll Flip, Charlie Brown
You're Something Else, Charlie Brown
Peanuts Treasury

PEANUTS.
TREASURY

by CHARLES M. SCHULZ

Foreword by Johnny Hart

HOLT, RINEHART AND WINSTON

New York • Chicago • San Francisco

Published simultaneously in Canada by Holt, Rinehart
and Winston of Canada, Limited.

Library of Congress Catalog Card Number: 68-24748

First published in October 1968

Third Printing, October, 1969

SBN: 03-072585-2
Printed in the United States of America

For Meredith, Monte, Craig, Amy, and Jill

Foreword

A lot of years ago, a man named Oog sketched a bison on a cave wall, and a bunch of neighbors that saw it first hand were blabbing it about that Oog could knock out a bison that looked like the real item. Needless to say, Oog was the hit of every cookout for many years to follow.

Hosts would clink their leftover bones to get the attention of their guests and give Oog a tremendous introduction. Then Oog would whip out his red sable and a can of blackberry juice and knock out a fast bison on a nearby rock. The guests would poke one another in the ribs with their massive elbows and say: "How about that . . . just like the real item, eh?"

Oog got a little carried away with all this and began putting oversized humps on the bison and giving them big feet and funny noses. People noticed right off that this didn't look like the real item, so they started hissing and booing, a little mannerism they picked up from observing snakes and ghosts. Oog got the message, but was unperturbed with his critics. In his heart he knew he was reaching for a new art form that they did not yet comprehend, so the hisses and boos only added fuel to the fire of his fervor.

It will probably come as no surprise to those of you who are reading ahead, that Oog's illustrious career was dramatically foreshortened. Indeed, many among you who have seen someone trampled to death by a herd of angry, big-footed bison with funny humps, a species which had not yet learned to laugh at themselves, may be unimpressed to a fault.

It is hard to say why humans are able to laugh at themselves and bison are not. Since the very beginning, each era or generation has had its satirical cartoonist; one who stands above the others, points to what we have really become, and teaches us to laugh.

Our time has given us the best yet. He is Charles M. Schulz and it is an honor, not easily described, to be asked to write this Foreword for my friend and idol, particularly for a work of such importance as the undertaking of this book. Charlie Schulz and the "Peanuts" gang inspired, eleven years ago, my own decision to enter the comic strip world. Charlie is a dear man who has taken it upon himself to make children of us all. Let us be eternally grateful for his foresight. We are God's children after all, and are meant to be no more than that. As a jealous child who loves to laugh, I sometimes, with growing understanding, resent the laughs that God must surely enjoy at the expense of his clumsy, faltering children. He shares, of course, an equal amount of sorrow, which I do not wish to get into. Charlie Schulz does get into this. He gives us our pathetic side, and we laugh with dewy eyes.

One evening I read a strip which has Charlie Brown hesitating before the principal's office. He prays for the strength to face his ordeal, then like most of us who are not quite sure of that "mustard seed" bewails, "My stomach hurts." My wife and kids had to pry me off the floor with an abalone iron on that one. The "stomach" strip now hangs on a wall in my studio. There are times when Charlie Brown and the red-headed girl cause me more tears than laughter. Not knowing whether to cry or laugh is, at its best, an exhilarating feeling. We've all felt it. The invariable result is laughter, which feels good.

Charlie Schulz is a man who not only knows the intricate parts of the funny bone, but proves his knowledge day by day. All things to Schulz contain the element of fun. You and I and the world can rest assured that the day cannot come when a herd of angry, pumpkin-headed kids trample Charlie Schulz; he has already seen to that. They walk around three feet off the ground. Don't take my word for it, turn the page . . . see for yourself.

JOHNNY HART

Endicott, New York
August 1968

PEANUTS TREASURY

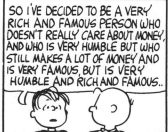

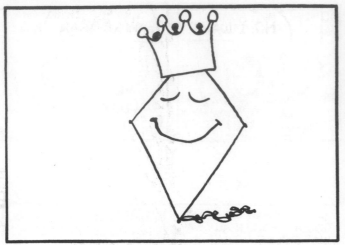

CHARLIE BROWN, YOU CAN'T POSSIBLY IMAGINE HOW GLAD WE'LL ALL BE WHEN THE KITE-FLYING SEASON IS OVER!

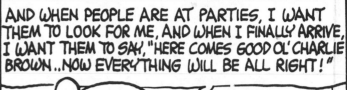

CHARLIE BROWN, I'VE BEEN FEELING AWFULLY GUILTY ABOUT NOT GIVING YOU A VALENTINE THIS YEAR...I'D LIKE FOR YOU TO HAVE THIS ONE

HOLD ON THERE! WHAT DO YOU THINK YOU'RE DOING? WHO DO YOU THINK YOU ARE?!

WHERE WERE YOU FEBRUARY 14th WHEN EVERYONE ELSE WAS GIVING OUT VALENTINES? IS KINDNESS AND THOUGHTFULNESS SOMETHING YOU CAN MAKE RETROACTIVE? DON'T YOU THINK HE HAS ANY FEELINGS?!

YOU AND YOUR FRIENDS ARE THE MOST THOUGHTLESS BUNCH I'VE EVER KNOWN! YOU DON'T CARE ANYTHING ABOUT CHARLIE BROWN! YOU JUST HATE TO FEEL GUILTY!

AND NOW YOU HAVE THE NERVE TO COME AROUND A WHOLE MONTH LATER, AND OFFER HIM A USED VALENTINE JUST TO EASE YOUR CONSCIENCE! WELL, LET ME TELL YOU SOMETHING... CHARLIE BROWN DOESN'T NEED YOUR...

DON'T INTERFERE...I'LL TAKE IT!

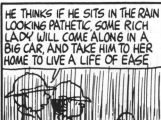

 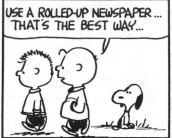  

IT'S A STORY I'VE BEEN READING CALLED "THE PIT AND THE PENDULUM" BY POE, AND IT'S ABOUT THIS MAN, SEE, WHO IS A PRISONER....

HE'S TIED TO A TABLE, AND THIS BIG PENDULUM KEEPS SWINGING BACK AND FORTH ABOVE HIM, GETTING NEARER AND NEARER...

IT SOUNDS LIKE AN EXCITING STORY..I'LL HAVE TO READ IT..

I THINK YOU'D ENJOY IT.. I REALLY DO...

THAT EDGAR ALLAN POE WAS A RIOT..

HELLO, KITE-EATING TREE!

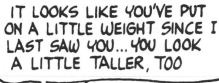

IT LOOKS LIKE YOU'VE PUT ON A LITTLE WEIGHT SINCE I LAST SAW YOU... YOU LOOK A LITTLE TALLER, TOO

BUT YOU HAVEN'T HAD ANY KITES LATELY, HAVE YOU?

WELL, YOU'RE NOT GOING TO GET **THIS** KITE, YOU DIRTY KITE-EATING TREE! I'LL FLY IT CLEAR OVER ON THE OTHER SIDE OF TOWN JUST TO SPITE YOU! YOU CAN STARVE, DO YOU HEAR?!

YOU'RE PRACTICALLY DROOLING, AREN'T YOU? YOU HAVEN'T EATEN A KITE FOR MONTHS, AND YOU'RE JUST DYING TO GET HOLD OF THIS ONE, AREN'T YOU? AREN'T YOU?

WELL, YOU'RE NOT, DO YOU HEAR ME? YOU'RE NOT!

HERE.. TAKE IT

IT'S BEEN A LONG WINTER, AND I'M VERY TENDER-HEARTED..

CHOMP! CHOMP! CHOMP!

WHAT IN THE WORLD ARE YOU DOING HERE?

PSYCHIATRIC HELP 5¢

I'M IN SAD SHAPE!

THE DOCTOR IS IN

MY LIFE IS FULL OF FEAR AND ANXIETY.. THE ONLY THING THAT KEEPS ME GOING IS THIS BLANKET...I NEED HELP!

WELL, AS THEY SAY ON T.V., THE MERE FACT THAT YOU REALIZE YOU NEED HELP, INDICATES THAT YOU ARE NOT TOO FAR GONE...

I THINK WE HAD BETTER TRY TO PINPOINT YOUR FEARS...IF WE CAN FIND OUT WHAT IT IS YOU'RE AFRAID OF, WE CAN LABEL IT...

ARE YOU AFRAID OF RESPONSIBILITY? IF YOU ARE, THEN YOU HAVE HYPENGYOPHOBIA!

I DON'T THINK THAT'S QUITE IT..

HOW ABOUT CATS? IF YOU'RE AFRAID OF CATS, YOU HAVE AILUROPHOBIA

WELL, SORT OF.. BUT I'M NOT SURE...

ARE YOU AFRAID OF STAIRCASES? IF YOU ARE, THEN YOU HAVE CLIMACOPHOBIA

MAYBE YOU HAVE THALASSOPHOBIA...THIS IS A FEAR OF THE OCEAN, OR GEPHYROPHOBIA, WHICH IS A FEAR OF CROSSING BRIDGES...

OR MAYBE YOU HAVE PANTOPHOBIA.. DO YOU THINK YOU MIGHT HAVE PANTOPHOBIA?

WHAT'S PANTOPHOBIA?

THE FEAR OF EVERYTHING..

THAT'S IT!!!

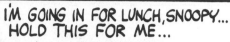
I'M GOING IN FOR LUNCH, SNOOPY... HOLD THIS FOR ME...

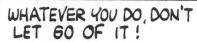
WHATEVER YOU DO, DON'T LET GO OF IT!

MAKE ONE MISTAKE, AND YOU PAY FOR IT THE REST OF YOUR LIFE!

SCHULZ

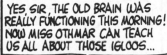

RATS! I FORGOT THE EGG SHELLS!

MISS OTHMAR WANTED US TO BRING SOME EGG SHELLS TO SCHOOL TODAY...WE WERE GOING TO MAKE IGLI...

IGLI?

THAT'S PLURAL, CHARLIE BROWN...

ONE IGLOO...TWO IGLI!

GOOD GRIEF! I FORGOT THE EGG SHELLS AGAIN!

MISS OTHMAR WILL BE SO UPSET! SHE WANTED US TO BRING EGG SHELLS TO SCHOOL TO MAKE A LITTLE IGLOO VILLAGE...

MISS OTHMAR TAKES HER JOB VERY SERIOUSLY...SHE DOESN'T EVEN LIKE TO BE CALLED A TEACHER...

SHE PREFERS TO BE CALLED AN EDUCATOR!

WOW! HOW SERIOUS CAN YOU GET?

WELL, DID YOU REMEMBER TO BRING THE EGG SHELLS TODAY, LINUS?

AS SOON AS I WOKE UP THIS MORNING, I THOUGHT TO MYSELF "HAVE MOM SAVE THE EGG SHELLS WHEN SHE FIXES BREAKFAST!"

SO?

SO TODAY WE HAD COLD CEREAL!

MISS OTHMAR GOT QUITE UPSET WHEN I TOLD HER I FORGOT THE EGG SHELLS AGAIN TODAY...

SHE TURNED SORT OF PALE AND PUT HER HEAD DOWN ON THE DESK...I THINK SHE MAY EVEN HAVE CRIED A LITTLE...

POOR MISS OTHMAR...I HOPE SHE DOESN'T BECOME ILL...

I NEVER REALIZED IT BEFORE, BUT A SCHOOL TEACHER IS A VERY DELICATE INSTRUMENT!

..AMEN!

AND PLEASE DON'T LET MISS OTHMAR CRACK UP..

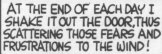

 ..AND SO THE OPHTHALMOLOGIST SAID I HAVE TO START WEARING GLASSES...

 AT FIRST I WAS PRETTY UPSET... IT WAS A REAL EMOTIONAL BLOW.. ALL SORTS OF THINGS WENT THROUGH MY MIND...

 BUT, FINALLY, ONE THOUGHT SEEMED TO STAND OUT.. / WHAT WAS THAT?

 IT'S KIND OF NICE TO BE ABLE TO SEE WHAT'S GOING ON!

 I'M SORRY THAT YOU HAVE TO WEAR GLASSES, LINUS...

 DON'T FEEL SORRY FOR ME, CHARLIE BROWN... WHY, I CAN SEE THINGS NOW THAT I NEVER KNEW EVEN EXISTED BEFORE!

 TAKE LUCY FOR INSTANCE... FOR THE FIRST TIME I REALIZE WHAT A GORGEOUS CREATURE SHE REALLY IS!

 GLASSES HAVEN'T IMPROVED ONLY HIS SIGHT... THEY'VE ALSO IMPROVED HIS SARCASM!

 WHEN I FIRST SAW LINUS WITH HIS NEW GLASSES, I COULD HAVE CRIED...

 I REALLY FELT SORRY FOR HIM.... WHEN HE CAME INTO THE HOUSE HE LOOKED LIKE A LITTLE OWL! IT JUST ABOUT BROKE MY HEART...

 ✳ SIGH ✳

 BUT IF YOU EVER TELL HIM I SAID SO, I'LL KNOCK YOUR BLOCK OFF!!

 HOW IN THE WORLD DID YOU EVER FIND OUT YOU NEEDED GLASSES?

 WELL, MY EYES USED TO WATER WHENEVER I TRIED TO READ AND EAT POTATO CHIPS, AND THEN ONE DAY I...

 YOU'RE LOOKING AT ME AS IF THIS WEREN'T A SCIENTIFIC EXPLANATION!

 YOU KNOW, IT'S VERY STRANGE...

 WHEN I FIRST GOT MY GLASSES, THEY KIND OF BOTHERED ME...

 I GUESS I JUST WASN'T USED TO THEM..

 NOW, I'M SOMETIMES NOT EVEN AWARE I HAVE THEM ON!

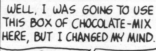

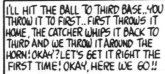

PAT PAT PAT

YOUR BROTHER PATS BIRDS ON THE HEAD..

WHAT?

ARE YOU OUT OF YOUR MIND?!

ARE YOU TRYING TO MAKE US THE LAUGHING STOCK OF THE WHOLE COMMUNITY?

HOW LONG DO YOU THINK WE'LL LAST AROUND HERE IF WORD GETS OUT THAT YOU PAT BIRDS ON THE HEAD?

NOW, CUT IT OUT!!

HOW ABOUT DOGS?

DOGS ARE ALL RIGHT...YOU CAN PAT ALL THE DOGS YOU WANT.. IN FACT, SOCIETY APPROVES OF PATTING DOGS ON THE HEAD!

THERE ARE MANY THINGS I DON'T UNDERSTAND..

SIGH

I SUPPOSE IF I TOLD YOU THERE'S A VULTURE OUTSIDE THAT'S BOTHERING ME, YOU'D SAY I WAS CRAZY, WOULDN'T YOU?

YES, I WOULD!

WHAT HAPPENED TO YOUR VULTURE?

HE'S NOT BOTHERING ME ANY MORE...HE GOT TREE SICK!

SCHULZ

IT'S A GOOD THUMB, BUT NOT A GREAT THUMB!

"SOON HANSEL AND GRETEL CAME TO A LITTLE COTTAGE"

"WHEN THEY GOT QUITE NEAR, THEY SAW THAT THE LITTLE HOUSE WAS MADE OF BREAD AND ROOFED WITH CAKE"

"THE WINDOWS WERE TRANSPARENT SUGAR"

THERE MUST NOT HAVE BEEN A VERY STRICT BUILDING CODE..

AMAZING!

THEY'VE FINALLY DEVELOPED A BONELESS CAT!

LOOK, HOW DO YOU EXPECT ME TO PRACTICE WITH YOU HANGING AROUND ALL THE TIME?

I'M SORRY.. I SHOULD HAVE KNOWN... I APOLOGIZE...

I'LL GO AWAY, AND LEAVE YOU ALONE...I UNDERSTAND YOUR PROBLEM COMPLETELY...

IT'S HARD TO CONCENTRATE IN THE PRESENCE OF A PRETTY FACE!

BOY, LOOK AT IT RAIN!

I'VE NEVER SEEN IT RAIN SO HARD FOR SUCH A LONG TIME..

I'M JUST GLAD I'M INSIDE..

WELL, GOOD GRIEF, ONLY A REAL BLOCKHEAD WOULD BE OUT IN A RAIN LIKE THIS...

WHERE IS EVERYBODY?

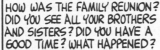

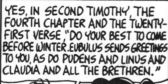

BONK

WHAT HAPPENED?
CHARLIE BROWN GOT HIT WITH A LINE-DRIVE!

DOES ANYONE HERE KNOW ANYTHING ABOUT FIRST-AID?
IT'S PROBABLY NOT SERIOUS.. SECOND OR THIRD-AID WILL DO

CHARLIE BROWN GOT HIT ON THE HEAD WITH THE BALL!
MERCY!

HERE, RUN OVER TO THE DRINKING FOUNTAIN, AND SOAK THIS HANDKERCHIEF IN COLD WATER...
YOU'RE KIDDING!

WITH A HEAD LIKE CHARLIE BROWN'S, YOU'LL NEED A BED SHEET!

I'M DYING, AND ALL I HEAR IS INSULTS!

WHAT HAPPENED?
YOU GOT HIT ON THE HEAD WITH A LINE-DRIVE, CHARLIE BROWN

I DON'T UNDERSTAND IT...

I USED TO BE ABLE TO DODGE THOSE LINE-DRIVES

WHEN YOU GET OLD, YOUR REFLEXES SLOW DOWN!

DON'T GET HIT WITH ANY MORE LINE-DRIVES, TODAY, CHARLIE BROWN
DON'T WORRY.. I FEEL SHARP!

POW!

SEE? I'VE GOT MY OLD REFLEXES BACK!

I'M ON A NEW CAMPAIGN TO BE NICE TO PEOPLE..

WHILE I'M AT IT, I SUPPOSE I MIGHT AS WELL INCLUDE DOGS..

HERE'S A NICE PAT ON THE HEAD..

THRILLSVILLE!

JOE SHLABOTNIK?

REALLY?

YOU HAVE A JOE SHLABOTNIK? YOU HAVE A JOE SHLABOTNIK BUBBLE GUM CARD?

HE'S MY FAVORITE PLAYER! I'VE BEEN TRYING TO GET HIM ON A BUBBLE GUM CARD FOR FIVE YEARS! YOU WANNA TRADE?

HERE...I'LL GIVE YOU WHITEY FORD, MICKEY MANTLE, ROBIN ROBERTS, LUIS APARICIO, BILL MONBOUQUETTE, DICK STUART AND JUAN PIZARRO!

NO, I DON'T THINK SO...

HOW ABOUT NELLIE FOX, DICK DONOVAN, WILLIE KIRKLAND, FRANK LARY, AL KALINE, ORLANDO PENA, JERRY LUMPE, CAMILO PASCUAL, HARMON KILLEBREW, BOB TURLEY AND ALBIE PEARSON?

NO, I DON'T WANT TO TRADE..I THINK JOE SHLABOTNIK IS KIND OF CUTE..

I'LL GIVE YOU TOM CHENEY, CHUCK COTTIER, WILLIE MAYS, ORLANDO CEPEDA, MAURY WILLS, SANDY KOUFAX, FRANK ROBINSON, BOB PURKEY, BILL MAZEROSKI, HARVEY HADDIX, WARREN SPAHN, HANK AARON, TONY GONZALES, ART MAHAFFEY, ROGER CRAIG, DUKE SNIDER, DON NOTTEBART, AL SPANGLER, CURT SIMMONS, STAN MUSIAL, ERNIE BANKS AND LARRY JACKSON!

NO, I DON'T THINK SO..

FOR FIVE YEARS I'VE BEEN TRYING TO GET A JOE SHLABOTNIK! MY FAVORITE BASEBALL PLAYER, AND I CAN'T GET HIM ON A BUBBLE GUM CARD... FIVE YEARS! MY FAVORITE PLAYER...

HE'S NOT AS CUTE AS I THOUGHT HE WAS!

TRASH

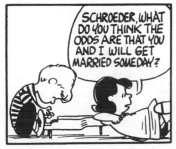

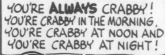

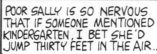

I'VE TAKEN ENOUGH OF YOUR INSULTS! C'MON, YOU AND I ARE GONNA FIGHT!

YOUR SUPPER'S READY, SNOOPY..I SET IT RIGHT OVER THERE IF YOU WANT IT...

C'MON, FORGET ABOUT EATING! FIGHT LIKE A MAN!

NO! I'M NOT GONNA SHAKE HANDS!

IF YOU WANT TO GET OUT OF THIS FIGHT, YOU'RE GOING TO HAVE TO APOLOGIZE BY KISSING MY HAND!

※SIGH※

I ACCEPT YOUR APOLOGY!

SMACK!

WHAT'S A LITTLE PRIDE WHERE YOUR STOMACH IS CONCERNED?

BLEAH!

YOU NEVER KNOW IN WHICH PART OF THE COUNTRY IT WILL HAPPEN..

ON HALLOWEEN NIGHT IN 1959 THE GREAT PUMPKIN APPEARED IN THE PUMPKIN PATCH OF BOOTS RUTMAN OF CONNECTICUT..

IF YOU DON'T BELIEVE ME, LOOK IN THE RECORD!

IN 1960 THE GREAT PUMPKIN APPEARED IN THE PUMPKIN PATCH OF R.W. DANIELS OF TEXAS...

AGAIN I SAY, IF YOU DON'T BELIEVE ME, LOOK IN THE RECORD!

NOW, SOMEWHERE IN THIS WORLD THE GREAT PUMPKIN HAS TO APPEAR THIS HALLOWEEN NIGHT!

WHY NOT HERE?!

MAYBE THIS PUMPKIN PATCH ISN'T BIG ENOUGH?

SIZE HAS NOTHING TO DO WITH IT! IT'S SINCERITY THAT COUNTS! ASK BOOTS RUTMAN! ASK R.W. DANIELS!

MAYBE IT'S NEATNESS, TOO...MAYBE HE APPEARS IN THE PUMPKIN PATCH THAT HAS THE LEAST WEEDS

NO, NO, NO, NO, NO, NO, NO! IT'S SINCERITY THAT COUNTS! THE GREAT PUMPKIN WILL APPEAR IN WHICHEVER PUMPKIN PATCH HE DECIDES IS THE MOST SINCERE!!

I'D HATE TO HAVE TO MAKE SUCH A DECISION!

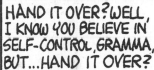

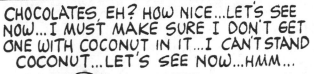

SCHULZ

Linus Van Pelt
ENGLISH I

SNOOPY, I'D LIKE TO READ YOU A STORY I'VE WRITTEN AND ILLUSTRATED FOR SCHOOL...

"ONCE THERE WAS A LITTLE GIRL WHO HAD A HEADACHE."

HER MOM GAVE HER SOME PILLS, BUT THEY DIDN'T HELP. HER MOM THEN TOOK HER TO THE DOCTOR.

"THE DOCTOR WAS UNABLE TO FIND ANYTHING WRONG."

"THIS IS A MYSTERIOUS CASE," HE SAID.

"THE LITTLE GIRL'S MOTHER TOOK HER HOME, AND PUT HER TO BED... HER HEAD THROBBED."

"HER LITTLE BROTHER CAME IN, AND SAID, 'MAYBE YOUR EARS ARE TOO TIGHT."

SO HE LOOSENED EACH EAR ONE TURN BACK. HER HEADACHE SUDDENLY STOPPED, AND SHE NEVER HAD ANOTHER HEADACHE AGAIN.

I GUESS HE DIDN'T LIKE IT.... THAT WAS HIS "GOOD LUCK, YOU'RE GOING TO NEED IT" HANDSHAKE!

SO HOW'S THE ECLIPSE?

MY HEART IS FULL ON THE DAY I FIRST GO OUT TO THE OL' BALL FIELD...

I LOVE THE SMELL OF THE HORSEHIDE, THE GRASSY OUTFIELD AND THE DUSTY INFIELD...I LOVE THE MEMORIES..THE HOPES...AND THE DREAMS FOR THE NEW SEASON..

AH! THERE IT IS! MY PITCHER'S MOUND...COVERED WITH TRADITION..

AND DANDELIONS!

YOU'RE NOT HAPPY, ARE YOU?

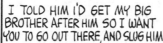

CHARLIE BROWN, THERE'S A BOY OUTSIDE WHO PUSHED ME DOWN...

I TOLD HIM I'D GET MY BIG BROTHER AFTER HIM SO I WANT YOU TO GO OUT THERE, AND SLUG HIM

YOU MEAN YOU WANT ME TO GO OUTSIDE, AND FIND OUT WHAT HIS PURPOSE WAS IN PUSHING YOU DOWN, AND ASK HIM NOT TO DO IT AGAIN..

NO, I WANT YOU TO GO OUT THERE, AND SLUG HIM!
THAT'S WHAT I WAS AFRAID OF...

THAT BOY OUTSIDE PUSHED ME DOWN, AND YOU'RE AFRAID TO DO SOMETHING ABOUT IT! A FINE BROTHER YOU ARE!

ALL RIGHT! I'LL GO OUT THERE! I'LL EITHER TEACH HIM A LESSON, OR GET MYSELF KILLED!

THAT'S THE SPIRIT !! "SYDNEY OR THE BUSH"!

"SYDNEY OR THE BUSH"?

I SUPPOSE YOU'RE ALL WONDERING WHY I'VE ASKED YOU HERE TODAY...

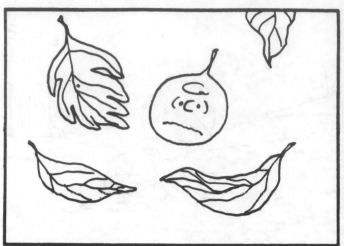

I HATE IT WHEN THE BASEBALL SEASON IS OVER

THERE'S A DREARINESS IN THE AIR THAT DEPRESSES ME...

EVERYTHING SEEMS SAD...EVEN THE OL' PITCHER'S MOUND IS COVERED WITH WEEDS...

I GUESS ALL A PERSON CAN DO IS DREAM HIS DREAMS...MAYBE I'LL BE A GOOD BALL PLAYER SOMEDAY...MAYBE I'LL EVEN PLAY IN THE WORLD SERIES, AND BE A HERO...

?

I BET I WILL PLAY IN THE WORLD SERIES SOMEDAY...I BET I'LL...

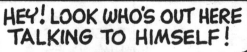

HEY! LOOK WHO'S OUT HERE TALKING TO HIMSELF!

WHAT ARE YOU DOING, CHARLIE BROWN, THINKING ABOUT ALL THE TIMES YOU STRUCK OUT?!

THERE'S A DREARINESS IN THE AIR THAT DEPRESSES ME!

SCHULZ

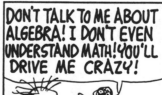

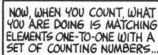

HE'LL BE LANDING ON TOP OF THE ROOF, YOU SAY?

WITH AN OVERLOADED SLED AND EIGHT REINDEER?

BOY, I DON'T KNOW....

I HAVE A FEELING HE'S GOING TO WISH HE HAD A LONGER LANDING STRIP!

THE ONLY WAY TO BEAT THE COLD WEATHER IS TO HIBERNATE..

I WILL NOW SETTLE DOWN IN MY DEN, AND NOT COME OUT UNTIL....

SUPPERTIME!

THAT WAS MY BLANKET-HATING GRANDMOTHER..

I WAS TRYING TO EXPLAIN WHY I NEED MY SECURITY BLANKET, BUT I JUST COULDN'T GET THROUGH TO HER..

WAS IT A BAD CONNECTION? YES

IT'S ALWAYS DIFFICULT TO TALK FROM ONE GENERATION TO ANOTHER

RATS!

I DON'T UNDERSTAND IT...

HOW COME SOME PEOPLE GET NO CHRISTMAS CARDS WHILE OTHER PEOPLE GET A WHOLE LOT OF THEM?

SOME OF US HAVE MORE FRIENDS

BUYING RECORDS CHEERS ME UP... WHENEVER I FEEL LOW, I BUY SOME NEW RECORDS..

I WAS SO DEPRESSED TODAY I BOUGHT MENDELSSOHN'S VIOLIN CONCERTO, BRAHMS' SECOND PIANO CONCERTO AND HANDEL'S ODE FOR ST. CECILIA'S DAY...

WOW!

HOW DEPRESSED CAN YOU GET?

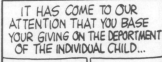
DEAR SANTA CLAUS,

IT HAS COME TO OUR ATTENTION THAT YOU BASE YOUR GIVING ON THE DEPORTMENT OF THE INDIVIDUAL CHILD...

IN OTHER WORDS, YOU JUDGE AS TO WHETHER THE CHILD HAS BEEN GOOD OR BAD...DO YOU REALLY THINK IT IS WISE TO ATTEMPT TO PASS SUCH JUDGMENT?

WHAT IS GOOD? WHAT IS BAD? CAN WE SAY TO OUR NEIGHBOR "YOU ARE BAD...I AM GOOD"? CAN WE SAY...
OH, BROTHER!

TO GO FURTHER INTO THIS MATTER OF THE GIFTS YOU BEAR, DEAR SANTA...

IF, PERCHANCE, YOU JUDGE A LITTLE CHILD AS TOO 'BAD' TO RECEIVE ANY TOYS, ARE YOU NOT ALSO JUDGING HIS PARENTS?

AND IF YOU JUDGE THE PARENTS, THEN ARE YOU NOT ALSO JUDGING THE REMAINDER OF THE FAMILY THE INNOCENT BROTHERS OR SISTERS, AS THE CASE MAY BE?

IN OTHER WORDS DEAR SANTA, MUST I SUFFER FOR THE DEEDS OF...
AH, HA!

I HEARD WHAT YOU WERE SAYING IN THAT LETTER! A FINE BROTHER YOU TURNED OUT TO BE!

LOOK, I WAS ONLY TRYING TO TELL SANTA CLAUS THAT I DIDN'T THINK HE SHOULD PASS UP OUR HOUSE, AND NOT LEAVE ME ANY PRESENTS JUST BECAUSE OF YOU!

IF HE THINKS YOU'VE BEEN BAD ALL YEAR, WHY SHOULD I SUFFER?

DON'T LOOK AT ME...I'M ONLY THE SECRETARY!

YOU AND YOUR LETTERS TO SANTA CLAUS!

YOU THINK YOU CAN GET ME IN BAD WITH HIM, BUT YOU CAN'T! SANTA IS VERY FORGIVING WITH LITTLE GIRLS!
OH, YEAH?

YEAH! LITTLE GIRLS CAN GET AWAY WITH A LOT MORE THAN LITTLE BOYS!
WHAT MAKES YOU THINK SO?

BECAUSE WE'RE SO CUTE!

I WORRY ABOUT THIS TIME OF YEAR...

I REMEMBER LAST YEAR ABOUT THIS TIME...IT WAS TWO O'CLOCK IN THE MORNING, AND I WAS SOUND ASLEEP...

SUDDENLY, OUT OF NOWHERE, THIS CRAZY GUY WITH A SLED LANDS RIGHT ON MY ROOF

HE WAS OKAY, BUT THOSE STUPID REINDEER KEPT STEPPING ON MY STOMACH!

OH, NO! DON'T TELL ME! NOT AGAIN!

HERE'S YOUR PIECE FOR THE CHRISTMAS PROGRAM..

"SO THE WORDS SPOKEN THROUGH JEREMIAH THE PROPHET WERE FULFILLED: 'A VOICE WAS HEARD IN RAMA, WAILING AND LOUD LAMENTS; IT WAS RACHEL WEEPING FOR HER CHILDREN AND REFUSING ALL CONSOLATION BECAUSE THEY WERE NO MORE.'" GOOD GRIEF!!

MEMORIZE IT, AND BE READY TO RECITE IT BY NEXT SUNDAY!

I CAN'T MEMORIZE SOMETHING LIKE THIS IN A WEEK! THIS IS GOING TO TAKE RESEARCH

WHO WAS JEREMIAH? WHERE WAS RAMA? WHY WAS RACHEL SO UPSET?

YOU CAN'T RECITE SOMETHING UNTIL YOU KNOW THE "WHO," THE "WHERE" AND THE "WHY"!

I'LL TELL YOU THE "WHO", THE "WHERE" AND THE "WHY"!

YOU START MEMORIZING RIGHT NOW, OR YOU'LL KNOW WHO IS GOING TO SLUG YOU, AND YOU'LL KNOW WHERE SHE'S GOING TO SLUG YOU AND YOU'LL KNOW WHY SHE SLUGGED YOU!!!

CHRISTMAS IS NOT ONLY GETTING TOO COMMERCIAL, IT'S GETTING TOO DANGEROUS!

Happiness is a Christmas vacation with no book reports to write.

DEAR SANTA CLAUS, HOW HAVE YOU BEEN?

PLEASE DON'T GET THE IDEA THAT I AM WRITING BECAUSE I WANT SOMETHING.

NOTHING COULD BE FURTHER FROM THE TRUTH. I WANT NOTHING.

IF YOU WANT TO SKIP OUR HOUSE THIS YEAR, GO RIGHT AHEAD. I WON'T BE OFFENDED. REALLY I WON'T.

SPEND YOUR TIME ELSEWHERE. DON'T BOTHER WITH ME. I REALLY MEAN IT.

WHAT IN THE WORLD KIND OF LETTER IS THIS?!!

I'M HOPING THAT HE'LL FIND MY ATTITUDE PECULIARLY REFRESHING

SCHULZ

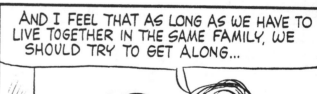

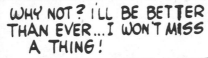

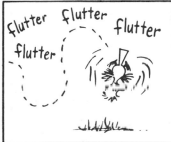

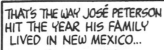

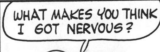

HEY!

LOOK AT THAT, WILL YOU?

WHAT'S THE MATTER?

THAT BIG KID JUST PUSHED DOWN THAT LITTLE RED-HAIRED GIRL! WHAT A BULLY!

SHE GOT UP....BUT, LOOK! HE'S GOING TO PUSH HER DOWN AGAIN!

OH, WHY AREN'T I TOUGH? WHY CAN'T I RUSH OVER THERE AND SAVE HER?

BECAUSE I'D GET SLAUGHTERED, THAT'S WHY! I'M NOT TOUGH... I'M NOT ANYTHING! I'M..

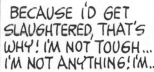

CRACK!

I'LL TAKE CARE OF HIM, CHARLIE BROWN!

CRACK!

YOU CAN RELAX, CHARLIE BROWN...HE WON'T BOTHER HER ANY MORE!

THAT'S VERY COMFORTING... I'M THE FRIEND OF A HERO!

AHEM!

!

RIGHT IN THE MIDDLE OF A BALL GAME?

ARE YOU OUT OF YOUR MIND?!
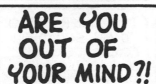

I'M TRYING TO PITCH, CAN'T YOU SEE THAT?!! I'VE GOT TO CONCENTRATE ON WHAT I'M DOING!

OH, NOW YOU'RE GOING TO BE HURT, AREN'T YOU? OH, GOOD GRIEF, ALL RIGHT... COME HERE...

SKRITCH SKRITCH SKRITCH SKRITCH SKRITCH

SIGH!

NO WONDER SANDY KOUFAX RETIRED!

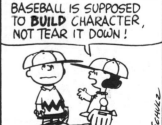

I'VE BEEN THINKING...

WHY COULDN'T I RUN OFF A FORM LETTER ON A STENCIL, AND SEND THE SAME LETTER TO THE 'GREAT PUMPKIN' SANTA CLAUS AND THE EASTER BUNNY?

I DON'T THINK THEY'D EVER KNOW THE DIFFERENCE.... I'M **SURE** THE 'GREAT PUMPKIN' WOULDN'T... HE'S VERY NAÏVE...

I WISH YOU HADN'T TOLD ME THAT... I'M DISILLUSIONED...

YOU MEAN YOU'RE GOING TO SEND THE SAME FORM LETTER TO THE 'GREAT PUMPKIN', SANTA CLAUS AND THE EASTER BUNNY?

WHY NOT? THOSE GUYS GET SO MUCH MAIL THEY CAN'T POSSIBLY TELL THE DIFFERENCE...

I BET THEY DON'T EVEN READ THE LETTERS THEMSELVES! HOW COULD THEY?!

THE TROUBLE WITH YOU, CHARLIE BROWN, IS YOU DON'T UNDERSTAND HOW THESE BIG ORGANIZATIONS WORK!

DEAR GREAT PUMPKIN, I AM LOOKING FORWARD TO YOUR ARRIVAL ON HALLOWEEN NIGHT.

I HOPE YOU WILL BRING ME LOTS OF PRESENTS.

EVERYONE TELLS ME YOU ARE A FAKE, BUT I BELIEVE IN YOU.
SINCERELY,
LINUS VAN PELT

P.S. IF YOU REALLY ARE A FAKE, DON'T TELL ME. I DON'T WANT TO KNOW.

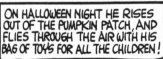
THIS IS THE TIME OF YEAR TO WRITE TO THE 'GREAT PUMPKIN'

ON HALLOWEEN NIGHT HE RISES OUT OF THE PUMPKIN PATCH, AND FLIES THROUGH THE AIR WITH HIS BAG OF TOYS FOR ALL THE CHILDREN!

I'M WRITING TO HIM NOW....DO YOU WANT ME TO PUT IN A GOOD WORD FOR YOU, CHARLIE BROWN?

BY ALL MEANS... I CAN USE ALL THE INFLUENCE I CAN GET IN HIGH PLACES!

AND ON HALLOWEEN NIGHT THE "GREAT PUMPKIN" RISES OUT OF THE PUMPKIN PATCH...

THEN HE FLIES THROUGH THE AIR TO BRING TOYS TO ALL THE GOOD LITTLE CHILDREN EVERYWHERE!

THAT'S A GOOD STORY...

I PLACE IT JUST A LITTLE BELOW THE ONE ABOUT THE FLYING REINDEER!

AS LONG AS SCHROEDER HAS QUIT THE TEAM, THE REST OF US ARE GOING TO QUIT, TOO!

IF HE CAN QUIT BECAUSE HE LIKES BEETHOVEN BETTER THAN BASEBALL, WE FEEL THAT WE HAVE A RIGHT TO QUIT, TOO!

GOOD GRIEF!

BEANED BY BEETHOVEN!

I'VE CAUSED YOU A LOT OF TROUBLE, HAVEN'T I, CHARLIE BROWN?

IF I HAD KNOWN THE WHOLE TEAM WAS GOING TO WALK OUT ON YOU, I NEVER WOULD HAVE QUIT

OH, IT'S NOT YOUR FAULT, SCHROEDER.. I DON'T BLAME YOU FOR WANTING TO PLAY THE PIANO INSTEAD OF BASEBALL...I'D PROBABLY DO THE SAME THING IF I WERE TALENTED..

AND SELFISH

WHY ARE YOU EATING SO MUCH CANDY, CHARLIE BROWN?

I'M EATING BECAUSE I'M FRUSTRATED, THAT'S WHY!

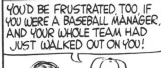
YOU'D BE FRUSTRATED, TOO, IF YOU WERE A BASEBALL MANAGER, AND YOUR WHOLE TEAM HAD JUST WALKED OUT ON YOU!

YES, I GUESS MAYBE I WOULD..

BUT I WOULDN'T BE SO CRABBY!

LIFE IS PECULIAR...

WOULDN'T YOU LIKE TO HAVE YOUR LIFE TO LIVE OVER IF YOU KNEW WHAT YOU KNOW NOW?

WHAT DO I KNOW NOW?

I WORRY ABOUT GETTING OLD...

THAT'S NOTHING TO WORRY ABOUT

OF COURSE, IT'S SOMETHING TO WORRY ABOUT...

WHO WANTS TO BE NINE?!!

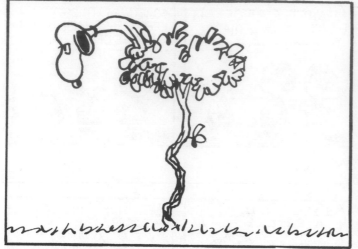
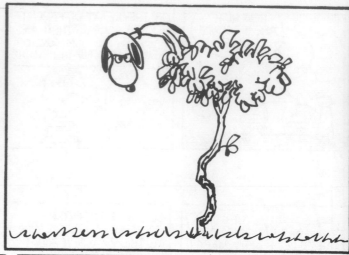

HERE'S THE FIERCE VULTURE SITTING HIGH IN A TREE WAITING FOR A VICTIM TO COME ALONG..

AH! A VICTIM APPROACHES! AS HE PASSES BY THE TREE, I SHALL SWOOP DOWN UPON HIM!

GET READY..... GET SET....

SWOOP!

KLUNK!

IF YOU'LL PARDON MY SAYING SO, YOUR "SWOOPING" LEAVES MUCH TO BE DESIRED...

MAYBE I COULD GO TO SWOOP SCHOOL...

SCHULZ

ORDINARILY, I FROWN ON CARD PLAYING, BUT BRIDGE IS A PRETTY GOOD GAME, AND, AFTER ALL, THEY DO NEED A PLACE TO PLAY...

"PASS"?!

SOME PEOPLE JUST SHOULDN'T PLAY CARDS TOGETHER!

LET'S SEE..WE'LL HAVE TO HAVE A STATION WAGON, A TOWN CAR AND A SPORTS CAR...OUR HOME SHOULD BE IN AT LEAST THE ONE-HUNDRED-THOUSAND CLASS... DO PIANO PLAYERS MAKE A LOT OF MONEY?

I DON'T KNOW...I SUPPOSE IT DEPENDS ON HOW HARD THEY PRACTICE...

I SEE..

WELL, I'LL PROBABLY NEED A HALF DOZEN FUR COATS, AT LEAST THIRTY SKI OUTFITS AND ABOUT FIFTY FORMALS...I'LL NEEDS LOTS OF JEWELRY AND EXOTIC PERFUMES AND I'LL NEED ABOUT A HUNDRED PAIRS OF SHOES...

WE'LL HAVE TO HAVE A SWIMMING POOL, OLYMPIC SIZE, HEATED, AND RIDING HORSES, A TENNIS COURT AND A HUGE FORMAL GARDEN...WE WILL TRAVEL EXTENSIVELY, OF COURSE; ROUND-THE-WORLD CRUISES...THAT SORT OF THING...AND...

KEEP PRACTICING, KID!

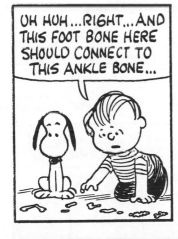

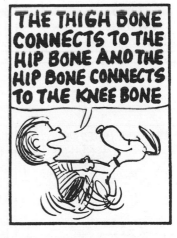
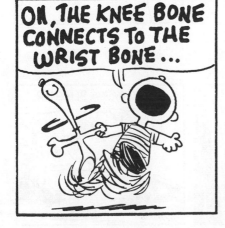

 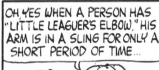   

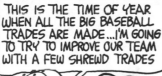

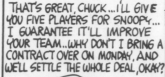

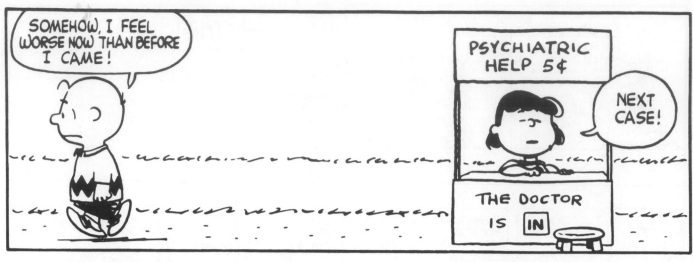

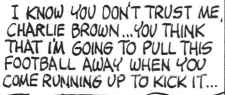

HERE IT IS...
THREE O'CLOCK...
"DOCTORS' ROUND TABLE"

WHAT ARE YOU WATCHING?

"MONSTER MADNESS"

I DON'T SUPPOSE YOU'D CARE TO WATCH "DOCTORS' ROUND TABLE"?

NO, I WOULDN'T!

THEY HAVE A GOOD PANEL TODAY.. A PHYSICIAN, A PHILOSOPHER, A THEOLOGIAN AND A DENTIST...

THEY'RE DISCUSSING, "WHERE CAIN GOT HIS WIFE AND THE IMPORTANCE OF A PRE-SCHOOL CHECK-UP"...

WELL, YOU MIGHT AS WELL FORGET IT BECAUSE I'M WATCHING "MONSTER MADNESS"!

I'LL GO OVER TO CHARLIE BROWN'S HOUSE...MAYBE HE'LL LET ME WATCH MY PROGRAM OVER THERE

HI, LINUS...COME ON IN...YOU JUST MISSED "DOCTORS' ROUND TABLE"

IT WAS PRETTY GOOD....THE PHILOSOPHER AND THE THEOLOGIAN AGREED THAT A PRE-SCHOOL CHECK-UP IS A VERY WISE ACTION...

WHERE HAVE YOU BEEN? YOU MISSED A REAL GOOD PROGRAM...

THE PHYSICIAN AND THE DENTIST GOT INTO A BIG FIGHT OVER WHERE CAIN GOT HIS WIFE!

SCHULZ

WHERE IN THE WORLD ARE YOU GOING?

I'M GOING TO SPEND THE NIGHT AT CHARLIE BROWN'S HOUSE..

DO YOU EVER HAVE PROWLERS AROUND HERE, CHARLIE BROWN?

WHY? ARE YOU SCARED?

OH, I'M ALWAYS SORT OF WORRIED ABOUT PROWLERS...

YOU FORGET THAT WE HAVE A WATCHDOG HERE...

YOU MEAN SNOOPY? IS HE A GOOD WATCHDOG?

I DON'T THINK THERE'S A BETTER ONE..

YOU'RE RIGHT...SEEING HIM OUT THERE ON GUARD MAKES ME FEEL A LOT BETTER!

TO THOSE OF US WITH REAL UNDERSTANDING, DANCING IS THE ONLY PURE ART FORM!

SOME DAYS I TASTE LIKE AN INFERIOR BRAND!

NO ONE WANTS TO TURN MY JUMP ROPE FOR ME..

THEY ALL SAY I'M TOO CRABBY..

THEY SAY I COMPLAIN TOO MUCH..THEY SAY I COMPLAIN WHEN THEY TURN IT TOO FAST AND THEY SAY I COMPLAIN WHEN THEY TURN IT TOO SLOW

NO ONE UNDERSTANDS US CRABBY PEOPLE!

CHARLIE BROWN, I WANT TO ASK YOU SOMETHING..

DO YOU THINK I'M A CRABBY PERSON?

YES, I THINK YOU'RE A VERY CRABBY PERSON

WELL, WHO CARES WHAT YOU THINK?!

MAYBE I AM TOO CRABBY...

MAYBE I SHOULD TRY TO BE NICER TO PEOPLE...

I SUPPOSE I COULD IF I REALLY TRIED..

OH, HOW I HATE TO GIVE THE REST OF THE WORLD THAT SATISFACTION!

SIGH!

I DON'T THINK I'D MIND SCHOOL AT ALL IF IT WEREN'T FOR THESE LUNCH HOURS...I GUESS I'LL SIT ON THIS BENCH...

I HAVE TO SIT BY MYSELF BECAUSE NOBODY ELSE EVER INVITES ME TO SIT WITH THEM...

PEANUT BUTTER AGAIN! OH, WELL, MOM DOES HER BEST...

THOSE KIDS LOOK LIKE THEY'RE HAVING A LOT OF FUN...I WISH THEY LIKED ME... NOBODY LIKES ME...

THE PTA DID A GOOD JOB PAINTING THESE BENCHES...

I'D GIVE ANYTHING IN THE WORLD IF THAT LITTLE GIRL WITH THE RED HAIR WOULD COME OVER, AND SIT WITH ME..

I GET TIRED OF ALWAYS BEING ALONE...I WISH THE BELL WOULD RING...

A BANANA...RATS! MOM ALWAYS...STILL, I GUESS SHE MEANS WELL...

I BET I COULD RUN JUST AS FAST AS THOSE KIDS.. THAT'S A GOOD GAME THEY'RE PLAYING...

THAT LITTLE GIRL WITH THE RED HAIR IS A GOOD RUNNER...

AH, THERE'S THE BELL! ONE MORE LUNCH HOUR OUT OF THE WAY...

TWO-THOUSAND, ONE-HUNDRED AND TWENTY TO GO!

AH! THE MOSELLE RIVER!

HERE'S THE WORLD WAR I PILOT DOWN BEHIND ENEMY LINES...

BY NIGHT I SNEAK THROUGH THE ABANDONED TRENCHES..

BY DAY I SLEEP ON HAYSTACKS...

SUDDENLY IT'S NIGHT AGAIN...I MUST CONTINUE MY JOURNEY ACROSS FRANCE TO REACH THE CHANNEL...

WHAT'S THIS? A SMALL FRENCH FARM HOUSE! ANYBODY HOME?

AH, MADEMOISELLE...DO NOT BE AFRAID..I AM A PILOT WITH THE ALLIES.. MY PLANE WAS SHOT DOWN BY THE RED BARON ...

SHE DOES NOT UNDERSTAND ZE ENGLISH...AH, BUT SHE WILL UNDERSTAND THAT I AM A HANDSOME YOUNG PILOT...

AND SHE? SHE IS A BEAUTIFUL FRENCH GIRL.. SOUP?AH,YES,MADEMOISELLE, THAT WOULD BE WONDERFUL! A LITTLE POTATO SOUP, AND I WILL BE ON MY WAY...

BUT HOW CAN I BEAR TO LEAVE HER? PERHAPS SOMEDAY I CAN RETURN..AU REVOIR, MADEMOISELLE..AU REVOIR! AH, WHAT A PITY...HER HEART IS BREAKING... DO NOT CRY, LITTLE ONE.. DO NOT CRY...

FAREWELL! FAREWELL!

CURSE THE RED BARON AND HIS KIND! CURSE THE WICKEDNESS IN THIS WORLD! CURSE THE EVIL THAT CAUSES ALL THIS UNHAPPINESS! CURSE THE..

I THINK THESE MISSIONS ARE GETTING TO BE TOO MUCH FOR HIM..

  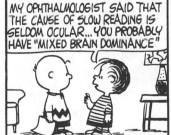 

 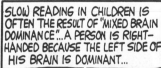   

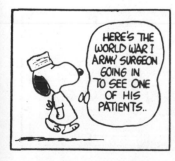